INSEMINATING THE ELEPHANT

BOOKS BY LUCIA PERILLO

Inseminating the Elephant

I've Heard the Vultures Singing: Field Notes on Poetry, Illness, and Nature

Luck Is Luck

The Oldest Map with the Name America: New and Selected Poems

The Body Mutinies

Dangerous Life

Inseminating
the Elephant

Lucia Perillo

Copper Canyon Press
Port Townsend, Washington

Copyright 2009 by Lucia Perillo

All rights reserved

Printed in the United States of America

Cover art: Jojo, "Off the Wall," 2004. Acrylic on paper, 22" × 20". Jojo, an eighteen-year-old male elephant, is a student at the Lampang Elephant Art Academy at the Thai Elephant Conservation Center in northern Thailand. A sweet-tempered, tuskless bull, Jojo has been painting for eleven years and plays harmonica in the Thai Elephant Orchestra. Artwork courtesy of Richard Lair.

Copper Canyon Press is in residence at Fort Worden State Park in Port Townsend, Washington, under the auspices of Centrum. Centrum is a gathering place for artists and creative thinkers from around the world, students of all ages and backgrounds, and audiences seeking extraordinary cultural enrichment.

LIBRARY OF CONGRESS CATALOGING-IN-PUBLICATION DATA

Perillo, Lucia Maria, 1958–
Inseminating the elephant / Lucia Perillo.
    p.   cm.
ISBN 978-1-55659-291-1 (hardcover)
I. Title.
PS3566.E69146I67   2009
811'.54—dc22

                                                                    2008044772

ISBN 978-1-55659-295-9 (softcover)

9 8 7 6 5 4 3 2

COPPER CANYON PRESS
Post Office Box 271
Port Townsend, Washington 98368

www.coppercanyonpress.org

For Hayden Carruth (1921–2008) for cheering me on.
And for James Rudy for picking me up.

ACKNOWLEDGMENTS

These poems first appeared in *The American Poetry Review, Hunger Mountain, Indiana Review, Margie, The Mid-American Review, Narrative, New England Review, Ninth Letter, Northwest Review, Ploughshares, Poetry, Poetry Northwest, Subtropics, Sycamore Review, Tin House, TriQuarterly,* and *Willow Springs.*

"Breaking News," which first appeared in *Hunger Mountain,* was published as a broadside by Stinehour Press.

I am grateful to the MacArthur Foundation and Claremont Graduate School for encouraging my work through their generous support. Thanks also to Tim Kelly, Hayden Carruth, Jane Mead, and Ben Sonnenberg for their willingness to read drafts of these poems. I also want to say (contrary to those who rant against the American medical machine) that I couldn't write anything at all were it not for the people who maintain my organic matter with such genuine concern. So thanks, docs.

And I thank the inmates at the Washington (State) Corrections Center for Women, who trained my dog.

Any idiot can face a crisis; it is this day-to-day living that wears you out.

CHEKHOV

Contents

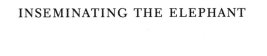

INSEMINATING THE ELEPHANT

Virtue Is the Best Helmet

One of these days I'm going to get myself an avatar
so I can ride an archaeopteryx in cyberspace —
goodbye, the meat cage.
Pray the server doesn't crash, pray
against the curse of carpal tunnel syndrome.

But then my friend the lactation consultant
brings up the quadriplegic who gave birth
(two times no less)
(motorcycle wreck)
just to make her body do
one thing the meat could still remember.

Somebody has to position the babies
to sip the breastmilk rivulets.
And the cells exude
despite their slumber. One minute
too much silence, the next there's so much screaming.

Turns out Madagascar's giant cockroach
makes a good addition to a robot
because the living brain adds up to more than: motor,
tracking ball, and the binary numeric code.

Usually the cockroach flees from light,
but sometimes it stands in its little coach unmoving,
stymied by the dumb fact of air.

And sometimes it rams into a wall
to force the world to show its hand.

Found Object

Somebody left this white T-shirt
like a hangman's hood on the new parking meter—
the magic marks upon its back say: *I QUIT METH 4-EVER.*
A declaration to the sky, whose angels all wear seagull wings
swooping over this street with its torn scratch tickets
and Big Gulp cups dropped by the curb.

Extra large, it has been customized
with a pocketknife or a canine tooth
to rough the armholes where my boobs wobble out
as I roam these rooms lit by twilight's bulb,
feeling half like Bette Davis in a wheelchair
and half like that Hells Angels kingpin with the tracheotomy.

Dear reader, do you know that guy?
I didn't think so. If only we could all watch the same TV.
But no doubt you have seen the gulls flying,
and also the sinister bulked-up crows
carrying white clouds of hotdog buns in their beaks:
you can promise them you'll straighten up, but they are such big cynics.

I should have told you *My lotto #'s 2-11-19-23-36*
is what's written in front, beside the silk screen
for Listerine Cool Mint PocketPaks™—
which means you can't hijack my name;
no, you have to go find your own, like a Hopi brave.
You might have to sit in a sweat lodge until you pass out

or eat a weird vine and it will not be pleasant. Your pulse
goes staccato like a Teletype machine—then *blam*

4

you'll be transformed into your post-larval being.
Maybe swallowtail, maybe moth: trust me, I know
because once I was a baby blue convertible

CopperCanyonPress.org

NO POSTAGE
NECESSARY
IF MAILED
IN THE
UNITED STATES

BUSINESS REPLY MAIL
FIRST-CLASS MAIL   PERMIT NO. 43   PORT TOWNSEND WA

POSTAGE WILL BE PAID BY ADDRESSEE

Copper Canyon Press
PO Box 271
Port Townsend, WA 98368-9931

Rebuttal

My quarrel with the Old Masters is: they never made suffering big enough—
that tiny leg sliding into the bay almost *insults* me,
that it should be all we get of the falling boy after the half-hour stunt
of his famous flying. *Don't you see*
they are cartoons? the drunk hissed
in the British Museum, a drunk in a sport coat
that made him look credible at first, some kind of docent,
an itinerant purveyor of glosses that left me
confused. I studied Brueghel's paintings, tiny
skaters, and hunters come home with tiny dead animals
gutted outside the frame, where the tiny offal
presumably had been left. I was looking for *Icarus*
but the *Musée des Beaux-Arts is in Belgium you twit*
and so I did not see the plowman wearing his inexplicably
dainty shoes, *a cartoon you American sow,*
and no one came to my rescue in that gallery vacated
even by its dust. Where I also did not see the galleon
anchored below the plowman's pasture with its oblivious,
content-with-being-tiny sheep. But just wait

until that ship sails out
and encounters the kind of storm that'll require Abstract
Expressionism to capture the full feeling of.
The giant canvases of the twentieth century!
Swaths of color with no figures in them at all!
How immense the drowning when you're the boy who drowns.
Between the fireball on your back and the water in front
all gray and everywhere and hard as concrete when you smack down.

"Dona"

Many of the Girl Scout songs
extorted a smile, our servile mugging—
but this one we loved best.
Starring a calf being hauled in a minor key,
its refrain two mournful syllables: *dona.*
First came the long *o*—an induction/seduction
to join the animal's cargo cult, then came
the short *a*, when the calf turned to beef
with no last meal and no reprieve.
The gist of the lyric: that we could choose
to be the calf in the cart or a bird in the sky;
the idea was simple, but also a lie: *dona.*
Bird is small and can fly where it wants
but it'll never be Miss Teen USA,
whereas the word *abattoir* was a chic French kiss
our tongues would enter willingly.
Let that bird flitter off
like a dry dead leaf: this was a hymn
that we sang on our knees
on the dais by the flag, dressed in our sashes
and green berets like irregulars planning
a suicide mission: there was glory ahead
when we signed on, clambered into the wagon,
and let the future hitch up its horse.

A Romance

I saw a child set down her binder like a wall
through the candy bin at the Corner Luncheonette
so she could scoop out gum while she spoke to the clerk—

and from that moment was in love: *Oh theft.*

College was supposed to straighten me
like a bent tree strangled by a wire,
but being done with sweetness I could not resist the lure of meat.

How the red muscle gleamed in its shiny wrap,
a wedge that had once been the thigh or the loin
of a slow brute's body, sugar-dirt and clotted grass

to be snatched in an instant
and zipped into the crone-y-est of pocketbooks.
Radiance housed in rawhide again, as when it was living.

A steak can be stuck in your jeans when you're skinny,
a rump roast is right for a puffy down coat,
small chops will fit under a thin peasant blouse

where it falls off the breasts
like a woodland river
with a limestone amphitheater underneath.

Ancient city, ancient sublet, ancient wooden fire escape—
with my other bandits I learned to say how-de-do in French.
We were yanking on the cord that would start the motor of our lives

though we did not have the choke adjusted yet.

Sometimes it seemed I floated in the dregs like a tea bag
bloating up with facts.
Until a girl ran in the door, panting hard, face red,

slab thudding
from her snowflake-damasked waist onto the table,
and we stood around it gawking at the way it seemed to breathe.

Notes from My Apprenticeship

COMPARATIVE MORPHOLOGY OF THE VERTEBRATES

Knowledge shipped north in white plastic buckets.
To pry the lid off was to open a tomb.
We began with the shark

and worked our way up through the frog and the dove—
each month we groped the swamp like fugitives
to raise the next ghoul on the syllabus.

With a bright blade I sliced through the pelt's wet mess,
exposing the viscera inside, tinted with latex
—blue for the veins, yellow for lymph—

it made me feel childish to see how far
somebody thought I needed the body to be
dumbed down. Outside was dumbed down

by late day's half-dark, as snowflakes dropped into
Lac Saint-Louis, paddled in silence by great northern pike,
their insides mangled by old hooks.

No place in them conformed to its
depiction in the charts, but the first lesson
was sameness: from the frog in one bucket

to the frog in the next—
no surprises ahead in the formaldehyde of my life:
obedient fugitive,

go on,
roll up your sleeve,
plunge your arm in.

WHITE RAT

Etherized in a bell jar, they resembled tiny sandbags, stacked

We carried each by its tail, their feet like newborn grappling hooks

Their insides had vaginal qualities, pink and wet and gleaming

The tissue hummed

My scalpel got jittery

I sewed up my rat as soon as I could

Because I realized the spiderwebstuff holding us here is thin

It was in fact difficult to account for all the people walking around not dead

I don't think I ever cut the gland I was supposed to, out

In the coming weeks, in lab-light, I made up little prayers-slash-songs

Like: *Please white rat*

Let me not have damaged you

You to whom I will be shackled all my years

You out of all your million brethren

If not genetically identical, then close

My rat went back to its Tupperware basin

With the cedar chips and the drinking bottle

That went *chingle chingle* whenever water was sipped

Which reassured me, knowing my rat was staying well hydrated

Though most of them languished

Which was, after all, their purpose

Though my rat stayed fat

Suggesting I'd botched the job of excising its adrenal

Not that its fatness saved it in the end

When all the living ones were gassed

Because the Christmas break had nearly come

Because of the deadline for the postmortem dissection

And time for the final roundup of facts

Oh rat

As you snuffle through your next incarnation

Say as my albino postman

Or my Japanese neurologist who taps her mallet on my knee

While I try not to visualize myself with your pink eyes and flaky scalp

Your scabrous tail especially

Because I have killed plenty of other things

But none of them have claimed me the way you did

THE TURTLE'S HEART

When we arrived, each belly-shell had a hole
whose clean edge signified that a power tool had been used
by the glamorous lab assistant
still wearing her goggles,
her long hair puffed up by the grimy rubber strap.

⌒·

When I looked down, there was the heart
bumping in the hole,
and when I looked sideways
my braid dipped in like a paintbrush.

⌒·

Summers I spent in a WPA hut
where the turtles lived outside in a mortared pit.
Their beaks would strain open
for the pink gobs of dog food
riding the tines of battered forks my job was to clamp
into the dark hands of juvenile delinquents from the city.

Once night a raccoon, or a fox, I don't know, climbed in
and opened the turtles as if they were clams
and left the hearts stretched on the ramparts
like surreal clocks —
even my thuggiest felon shivered as they ticked.

⌒·

Little motorized phlegm-ball, little plug of chewing gum,
your secret is your frailty
once your outer walls are breached.

Makes me think of that submarine buried under the sea,
the sailors banging on the pipes
as if the water had ears.

Back in the lab, we fished up from the hole
the muscle's pointy end and tied it
to an oscillograph whose pen-arm moved at first in even sweeps.
Until a drop
of substance X made the graph go wild—
the heart scrawling in its feral penmanship
see what little of yourself you own.

DENVER WILDLIFE RESEARCH CENTER

The coyotes had to eat, which was the reason for the few bedraggled sheep kept in a pasture by the freeway.

We entered wearing coveralls stamped *Property of the United States,* the crotch of mine holstering my knees, while my tall boss strained the hem of his armpit when he lifted his pistol.

The sheep fell hard, as though she dropped a long way down.

He strung her up by her feet on the fence and commenced sawing with a buck knife, to expose the entrails that shined like a bag of amber marbles.

These he tore out and threw into a bucket, before pinching off the bladder and spilling it by the fence, where steam rose from a patch of crusted snow.

You can throw up if you want to, he said, and, because I'd been given no job but to carry a pail, I understood this to be a kind of test.

A test to let him know what kind of daughter I would be: dogged, like a coyote, or meek, like the sheep, when, later, we would lace the carcass with poison to find out how much was needed to leave half the coyotes dead.

(Another test, the LD50: LD for *lethal dose.*)

More sheep-daughter than dog-daughter, I did not think about the coyotes who paced along the chain-link of their cages or about the barn owls who lived tethered to their boxes in a field of wild asparagus.

Instead of thinking I was making sure I didn't throw up and didn't faint, even though the insides of the sheep were hotter than I expected and smelled more sweet.

THE CHAMBER

As does the poem by William Blake, this involves a poison worm,
    a worm that would make the blackbird who ate it
        flap and squawk in distress

while at regular intervals I played a tape of a bird
    also squawking in distress, so you see
        there was this salt-box-girl regression going on

while I took notes: *Now the bird is squawking in distress,*
    my job being to watch on closed-circuit TV
        and record the bird's death, were that to occur

in the chamber made from a gutted fridge
    rigged up to a button in the next room
        where, when I pushed, I'd hear a musical *plink*

over the loudspeaker as a mealworm dropped
    from a crown of vials that sat on the chamber,
        the crown rotating as the glass vials tipped,

one worm per plink, though I sometimes plinked twice
    if the worm got stuck
        or if the bird failed to squawk

in that tiny brick building that rustled with wings
    from birds scritching in cages
        I'd been filling for weeks,

my truck full of traps I set on fence posts at dawn,
    when the redwings clung
        to tall blades in the ditches

and sang *shuck-shreeek* as the dirt road fumed
    behind me in the mirrors, while ahead bore a rising
      red-winged sun that I drove into

feeling immortal,
    how could I not feel immortal
      when I was mistress of the poison worm?

SUPER 8

There were so many black birds I could not count,
homing on this patch of dusk. My boss's idea
had been to spray them with spangles
so that, if found, the finder would know
the bird had stopped here at this cornfield
behind the Super 8 motel. That is,
if he could imagine the helicopter
with its tank of glue and light.
Otherwise, he might just wonder at a spangled bird.

We untangled them from the mist nets
and brought them into the bathroom's white-tile grid
thirty feet east of the blacktop stripe,
where I counted the spangles, a soldier
in the tribe of useless data. Afterward
I walked them back outside two at a time
and opened my fists, where the birds paused
just long enough to leave their own data on my palms.
Here's what we think of
your spangles, your starlight. Then the night flushed
them up into its swoon—however faintly,
the corn glittered as the birds resumed their ravening.

IN VITRO/IN VIVO

Only once did the frog come to mind: when the coroner
came to "first-aid training" at the fire station,
his slide carousel set up to eliminate
the easy pukers. The frog was not dead
but its brain had been pithed, which is what happens
when you stick a probe into the skull and wiggle.
You wind up with something dead enough
to let you stretch its tongue as thin and wide
as a cellophane sheet, which I did so
eagerly, back in the lab. The coroner said:
Here is the fat guy whose Chihuahua
gnawed through his stomach. Click.
Here is the farmer who hanged himself in his silo.
(I noted his foreshortened dangling feet.) Click.
It had been thrilling to see the frog's blood cells
jerking through the narrow capillaries. Here
is the woman who swallowed the bottle of Drāno.
Click. Here is the man who just Sawzall-ed
his neck clean through. Click. Here is the guy
who shot off his head, but wait: he's still living,
which is what happens if the brain stem's left intact.
Click. The coroner said we should aim for the base
not the top of the skull and remember to turn down
the heat. Click. There are many people in this world
on whom nobody checks in very often. Click.
The warmer the room, the quicker a body
will turn black and bloat. Click.
If you have a dog it is important to leave out
what seems like an inordinate amount of dog food.
Click, click, then there was nothing

but a slab of light to signal he was through.
And it was then that I remembered the frog,
not that the coroner had spoken of frogs.
What he said was,
If we saw the cops outside, smoking cigars,
that's when we'd know we had a stinker.

SIMILAR GIRL

Most of the hospital's emergencies lay
on gurneys that made a chickadee noise —
eent eent eent — as they rolled on rubber wheels.

But the girl with the bellyache just walked in
clinging tight to her purse, protecting the pain,
as if she feared its being kicked.

Meanwhile an old woman whimpered in the next room
help me, god help me — here's the main thing I learned:
if trouble comes with an odor,

everyone scrams. That's how it was in the ER
where I ghosted the halls, for the red appliqué
the college ambulance corps wore on its sleeve —

I would rescue the beauties
who jumped off the campus walkway bridge
and lay on the pavement like old flowers pressed in books.

In the kitchenette lounge, one surly doc asked:
So who's going to tell her she's knocked up?
— cut to the girl who'd been waiting for hours

lit by a long bulb flickering out.
As for the doctors, well it would be easy
to harp on their chuckling, or sneer at the gum

they snapped with the vampire prongs of their teeth
or the way they used cold half-cups of coffee
to drown their cigarettes. But it was they

who called me to press on the man
whose heart had run through the course of its years,
millions of spasms in the box of his ribs —

later, on my doughnut napkin
I would calculate: a quarter billion.
And though they made fun of the similar girl,

they brought in a step stool for me to climb on
for the minutes required for their clean consciences
to declare him dead. (Six.) Their jimmy-legs tapped

as they studied the clock, while I studied the chest
bending under my palms
while the old woman cried *help me, god help me,*

and the young one hugged her purse like a doll
while *tick tick tick*, the miraculous ticking of ticks:
life ratcheted up inside her.

Two of the Furies

The old woman in the parking lot
wields her walker not unspryly. Gray hair
lank and without style, hanging
under her ski hat, as I wear a ski hat—
her legs bare under her skirt,
my legs bare under my skirt,
she wears sneakers, I wear sneakers—
windbreaker, windbreaker. She rolls up
to watch me board, as people do,
because it is *interesting*
to see the wheelchair maneuvered backward
into the van. *You got it?*
she asks, as people do
though I am not their child.
We are not sisters either,
despite the wind's ruffling our skirts in sync—
oh how she is interested in the ruffling of my skirt.
The ruffle makes her giddy, starts
her bald gums racing on their wordless observations
as she peers into my thighs.
How alike we are! says this
no-sister of mine to be argued with,
just some crazy old woman
flashing the terrible crater of her smile
to raise the wind and
prove her point.

Juárez

At night the bones move where the animals take them,
bones of the girls that once were girls,
the hand-bones missing, you know how it goes,
you fill in the blank, the unimaginable X
of horrid futures. From bus stops
before dawn, from outside the maquiladoras
when the horizon bites the sun's gold coin,
from the hundred places to fail to arrive at
or return from, the bones uncouple
their linkages and travel separate ways.
Too many of them for just one theory—
too many skulls for the drug lords even,
for the husbands the satanists the cross-border whore-killers
…until you start to suspect the dirt itself.
Between the concrete wall and the drainage ditch,
the sheet-metal scraps and collapsed storm fence,
a desert of ocotillo scrub, not even one decent
cowboy cactus, one bent arm
swearing an oath of truth. When I was younger
I wrote this poem many times and don't know
where I was going with it: so much worship
for every speck of mica giving off
a beam I made into a blade. And you can see
how I turned mere rocks into villains
when it turns out the landscape's not at fault,
the parched land a red herring—this is not the song
of how the men fried while hiding inside the boxcar
(and even then someone outside locked the door).
My poems took place where the wind-skids sang:
perhaps I've been too fond of railroad tracks

and the weedy troughs alongside them, which do
accept most everything. Especially the spikes,
how I loved those spikes cast into silence,
in this case behind the factories, where the grass
grows sparser than in the poor soils of Texas,
a place with completely different ghosts
lying just over the river. To get there
you will have to pass by a large pink cross
made out of such spikes at the border station,
and here's the main thing, forgive me, I missed in my youth:
how from each spike hangs a name.

Incubus

While the spectacular round butt of the fat junkie sitting on the curb
rotated upward from his belt—

the legs of the skinny junkie wriggled upward from a dumpster.
And when he stood, I saw
his familiar figure, thinned—

two times he'd snipped my kitchen with the scissors of his hips
while he directed stories from the rehab clinic toward us
ladies in our panty hose,

our fingers sliding up and down our wineglass stems.

Later, in the cloak of his jean jacket,
he slipped upstairs and stole my pharmaceuticals,
my legitimate pharmaceuticals!—

so an awkwardness descended on the realm of gestures
there in the alley behind the YMCA, where I looked at any alternate—
pothole, hydrant, not buttocks,
don't look at buttocks, don't look at dumpster, don't. Look:

I would have been a crone to him,
and he would have been my pirate son,
my son who sleeps beneath the bridge

in the cloak of his jean jacket, dabbed with fecal matter now.

Still, when he comes at night,
brass button by button
and blade by blade—his skinny thighs—

I open myself like a medicine cabinet
and let him take the pill bottles from my breasts.

First Epistle of Lucia to Her Old Boyfriends

Not infrequently I find myself wondering which of you are dead
now that it's been so long since I have had a boyfriend
for whom this wonder would be a somewhat milder version of
the way our actual parting went—i.e., with me not wondering
but outright wishing that an outright lightning bolt
would sail sharply into your thick heads.

Can I plead youth now over malign intent?
And does my moral fiber matter anyhow
since I have not gone forth and et cetera'd—
i.e., doesn't my absent children's nondepletion of the ozone layer
give me some atmospheric exchange credits under the Kyoto Protocol
to release the fluorocarbons of these unkind thoughts?

Anyhow what is the likelihood of you old boyfriends reading this
even if you are not dead? Be assured your end is hypothetical.
Also be assured I blush most furiously
whenever that tower room in Ensenada comes to mind
where the mescal functioned as an exchange credit for those lies you told
about your Alford pleas and your ex-wives who turned out not ex at all.

Anyhow the acid rain has caused my lightning to go limp
over bungalows where you have partial custody of your teenagers
and AA affirmations magneted to the fridge
from which your near beers sweat as you wonder if I'm dead,
since the exchange for this-here wonder is your wonder about me.
Even though it shows my nerve—to think you'd think of me at all—

I await word of your undeadness

P.S. along with your mild version of my just reward.

Raised Not by Wolves

The family sank into its sorrows—
we softened like noodles in a pot.
Whereas the bicycle's bones were painted gold
and stood firm against the house
no matter how hard it rained.

Beneath the handlebar mount, it said ROYAL in red letters
unscathed despite the elements;
this was the bicycle's first lesson,
to be royal and unscathed—

I pressed my ear-cup to the welds.

Pedal furiously, then coast in silence.
You will need teeth to grab the chain.
Exhortations with the stringent priggishness of Zen,
delivered by a guru who hauls you off and wallops you

in answer to your simple question.

Though its demise is foggy,
I can conjure with precision its rebukes, the dull sting
when the boy-bar bashed my private place.

Then no talking was permitted
beyond one stifled yelp.

You could, however, rub the wound
with the meat of your thumb—so long
as you did this stealthily, pretending you had an itch.

Amphicar

Amphicar rolls across the breakfast table
as the happy family plunges into the river—
don't worry. I've just trolled them from the river

of human news. Today's *lifestyle feature:*
this convertible that once topped my desires,
all my crackpot desires

(my parents would not buy one to drive the filthy current).
Instead we rode a station wagon into our oblivion,
when we could have ridden into our oblivion

with the means of rescue. In the famous myths
how many souls got banished to the underworld
(or turned into trees, their arms the branches whorled)

and were doomed because they let themselves be driven
over death's river (or into the tree)
without a plan for their re-entry

into living human form? In my actual river I never stepped down
because, the myth went, its bottom was shit,
and when the mayor confessed it *was* actual shit

the world proved itself to be a sluice of lies
even if the water was blue
or sort of blue.

Amphicar would have wheeled right through it,
manufactured '61 through '68, the years of my youth
(my banished-to-the-back-of-the-station-wagon youth),

with no propeller or white leather seats,
no top rolled down, no fishing pole slanting up.
No one listened to me: how we could just drive up

on the shores of Hell, and tan on that beach for a while.
If we only had an Amphicar. Then when we grew sick for home
we could have crossed back home.

Job Site, 1967

Brick laid down, scritch of the trowel's
downward stroke, another brick set
then the flat side of the trowel moving
across the top of the course of bricks.
My father stepped from the car in his brown loafers,
the rest of him is fading but not his loafers,
the round spot distended by his big toe.
Brick laid down, scritch of the trowel's
downward stroke, the silver bulb of the door lock
sticking up as I sat in the car,
the kid in the dress. Newark burned
just over the river, not so far south
as the South of their skin — deepening
under the ointment of sweat, skin and sweat
they'd hauled from the South
brother by brother and cousin by cousin
to build brick walls for men like my father
while Newark burned, and Plainfield burned,
while the men kept their rhythm, another brick set,
then the flat side of the trowel moving
across the top as my father crossed the mud.
I sat in the car with the silver bulb of the door lock
sticking up, though I was afraid,
the kid in the dress, the trowel moving
across the top of the course of bricks.
You can't burn a brick,
you smashed a brick through a window,
the downward stroke, another brick set,
but to get the window first you needed a wall,
and they were building the wall,

they were building the wall
while my father, in his brown loafers,
stepped toward them with their pay.

Wormhole Theory

Mario Perillo has died, call him Mr. Italy—
and I regret never having gone sightseeing
in a bus marked PERILLO TOURS.
He was no relative of mine,
all that connects us is the name:
this foldout plastic promotional rain hat
someone handed me at birth.
An accident of the alphabet: can't say
I haven't craved a more streamlined form—sometimes
you get tired of being Lucia Perillo
and want to slide by, without ripping the ether
with all your cognominal barbs and hooks.
Anthony DiRenzo, my old cubicle-mate,
went by the name of Mr. Renz—
a truncation that once caused my scorn to sputter forth,
though now I see: the burden of the vowels.
First there's the issue of the sonic clang
and next there's the issue of our guilt,
that we've strayed onto turf where we don't belong,
so far from the outer-borough homelands
of shoe repair and autobody shops.
This is the guilt Verdi captures in his aria
"Di Provenza il mar," which Anthony sang
one night in our empty basement office
while snow spread its hush money two floors above.
Alfredo's father is begging him to come home,
to abandon the floozy he picked up in Paris—
if he waits a hundred years, he can hop
aboard Mario's red-and-green tour bus
in time for the cocktail hour, perhaps,

with honeydew melon served the way I love it:
wrapped in the paper-thin slices of fat
that choked my father's heart.
Sometimes a name seems our most arbitrary possession,
and sometimes it seems like the grain in a rock
like a sculptor's hunk of Italian marble: whack it
and you might get either your first glimpse of a saint
or a pile of rubble. Now Mario P.
has entered my obituary book
facing Lucia Pamela, another tour guide of sorts,
having recorded her album on the moon
after flying there in her pink Cadillac.
One nutty broad, Mario would say: *A real fruity-patootie* —
whose off-key canzone-ing would plink in my ears
way too unsweetly this time of the morning
as Verdi holds forth through the hi-fi speakers
with another (*true story*) Lucia-of-the-vowels
singing the role of Alfredo's beloved slut.
In my own flights of grandeur, I am a wormhole
connecting the Roman Empire to outer space,
joining the Old World to the dogs on the moon —
however crudely my name has roughed me in.
In my hometown, Perillos were common as shrubs,
a tribe in white lipstick and lamb-chop sideburns,
such as worn by the one who spirited me to the docks
in the spaceship of his Nova. He even wore
my dad's middle name, and I bet the vortex of his lips
meeting mine would have ripped the cosmic silk
or caused a galactic cymbal crash. Or blown
the head gasket of the space-time bus:
sing *Tuscany Mercury Verdi Prosciutto* —
hail Mary, just Mary, three times for my penance
and thank the aniseed liquor for blacking me out.

Avoidance Behavior

The square watermelons that sell for ninety-two dollars in Japan
show up next to a painting by Congo the chimpanzee,
which sold for twenty-six thousand dollars yesterday,
though by *yesterday* I don't mean "yesterday"
because Congo died of tuberculosis forty years ago

and this newspaper is two months old,
and who knows where you (*hypothetical reader*) lie
if-anywhere in the future? You'll have to add X
to all the numbers as time passes
because the prices usually inflate

while space collapses around these things that hum as if with current,
until they're placed so close sparks arc across
and make my dental fillings zing.
And though matter is supposed to fly outward for X more billion years
(minus the time-space between me ≠ you)

flick the remote or
turn the page of the *Seattle Post-Intelligencer* —
and this melon turns into a mouse grafted to a human ear,
suggesting we've hastened the constriction
of the final falling-in. Yet

might not all this juxtapositional cram-it-all-in-ness
be our sly protest against the flying-out?
As in the new craze called *sacred snuggling*
where bodies touch, but do not rub
any membrane that might lubricate?

Wishful thinking? This belief
that we'll move toward the smell of sweat and scalp
when the giant meteor comes at last
or the bomb slants across the laundry lines ($\neq$) —
whatever the accelerant of our demise?

Me,
I'd rather be immersed, that's how far my matter's scattered,
that I'd leave all you behind
to skinny-dip in darkness at the end,
touched by nothing but a spring-fed lake.

Postcard from Florida

After paddling out, I found the manatees
in canals behind the pricey homes,
as I once found the endangered Hawaiian goose

beside the hulks that once were dream cars.
So the scarce beast gets its camouflage
at the farthest outpost of our expectations:

the gators prefer golf courses to marshes,
prefer Cheetos, Fritos, nachos, Ho Hos
to baby fish as bright as coins.

What doesn't kill us makes us strong
(see the scar where propellers have cut through the hide),
but doesn't that mean some of us *will* be killed

and not made strong? My sweet flabbies
swing their gum-rubber hips in freshwater
murmuring from the air-conditioning compressors

and waggle my little boat with their bristles —
what doesn't tip us over
makes us give a whopper sigh.

Look up, and a geezer by his pool
feeds a great blue heron from his hand:
they are so alike they could be twins, him croaking

a tune the bird has come to know
and stalks at certain times of day.
Meanwhile two girls next door in bathing suits

who have turned on the hose in their backyard
hop now at the edge of their wooden bulkhead
singing *Come to us humanities*

and oh see how they do.

Transcendentalism

The professor stabbed his chest with his hands curled like forks
before coughing up the question
that had dogged him since he first read Emerson:
Why am I "I"? Like musk oxen we hunkered
while his lecture drifted against us like snow.
If we could, we would have turned our backs into the wind.

I felt bad about his class's being such a snoozefest, though peaceful too,
a quiet little interlude from everyone outside
rooting up the corpse of literature
for being too Caucasian. There was a simple answer
to my own question (how come no one loved me,
stomping on the pedals of my little bicycle):

I was insufferable. So, too, was Emerson I bet,
though I liked *If the red slayer think he slays* —
the professor drew a giant eyeball to depict the Over-soul.
Then he read a chapter from his own book:
naptime.
He didn't care if our heads tipped forward on their stalks.

When spring came, he even threw us a picnic in his yard
where dogwood bloomed despite a few last
dirty bergs of snow. He was a wounded animal
being chased across the tundra by those wolves,
the postmodernists. At any moment
you expected to see blood come dripping through his clothes.

And I am I who never understood his question,
though he let me climb to take a seat

aboard the wooden scow he'd been building in the shade
of thirty-odd years. How I ever rowed it
from his yard, into my life — remains a mystery.
The work is hard because the eyeball's heavy, riding in the bow.

Final Leap

When the Black Elvis takes the stage, five of him appear —
start with the man in his white jumpsuit,
then add the jumbo projection behind,
throw in a replication of his replicated feet
plus two copies of his shadow. Though he is five,

he has never been ranked #1
because he does not look like Elvis, which is true:
his voice is more soulful than anyother Elvi
but the judges at the yearly Memphis finals
will not close their eyes and make that final leap.

Not so for the women here, who can frog
the leap still one bounce farther
until a spirit descends and the dead man
lives. It is a little troubling
how much the pageant resembles a Catholic mass

when the women approach as he descends
the stage's steps, bell-bottoms aflutter
around the doves of his white boots.
Then he drapes a satin strip around their necks.
Then comes the Amen of their swoons.

As for me, I don't see why a spirit
would deign to enter the body again
when you consider bloat colitis amphetamines etc.
and the final humiliations of the toilet.
Me, I'd prefer to be housed in a ghost

as I'd also prefer that Robert Washington
not wear the electric guitar around his neck
when it is not plugged in. But the scarves
have plugged in these women, who sound
as if they too have been amplified by five, forming one

big animal body my soul just might deign
to descend into. For the plain speech
of its snarls and yips: we are housed
in fur and we're housed in heat—
we are dogs tied to trees, at the end of a leap

before the lights come up and we are yanked back by our chains.

NOTE: Robert Washington did win the 2003
Images of Elvis contest, after I wrote this poem.

January/Macy's/*The Bra Event*

Word of it comes whispered by a slippery thin section
of the paper, where the models pantomime unruffled tête-à-têtes
despite the absence of their blouses.

Each year when my familiar latches on them so intently
like a grand master plotting the white queen's path,
like a baby trying to suckle a whole roast beef,

I ask: What, you salt block, are you dreaming
about being clubbed by thunderheads? — but he will not say.
Meanwhile Capricorn's dark hours flabbed me,

uneasy about surrendering to the *expert fitter*
(even if the cupped hands were licensed and bonded) —
I had August in mind, seeing the pygmy goats at the county fair.

Now the sky is having its daily rain event
and the trees are having their hibernal bark event,
pretending they feel unruffled

despite the absence of their leaves. And we forget how they looked
all flouncy and green. Instead we regard
fearfully the sway of their old trunks.

Odor Ode

Big stink wobbles down the library aisles
from you endomorphs who've come in from the thorns —
your musk percolates the picture books
while children sing to the donkey Tingalayo.

It creeps into the reference nook
and biographies of despot popes,
the manuals on car repair, even the old edition *Joy of Sex*,
the one whose hairy armpits haunt me.

How will the smudge of rotten leaves
ever be lifted from so many paperbackèd bosoms,
the baby doze peacefully in its holster, the ancestors spring
from the accordion-files in their old hats?

Outside, the slacker deer refuse to rut
ever since your scent made its bed on the lawn,
the Chamber of Commerce outraged and
the mayor mowing down the brambles.

Sleep safe here, men! — with your heads tipped back,
wooden newspaper spindles across your chests like swords
while those good Samaritans the moths
knit scarves from the wool of your loud roars and whistles.

Viagra

Let the dance begin.

In magazine-land, you two are dancing—
though a moment ago you were engaged
in some activity like stringing fenceline
or baling hay—why else the work gloves
sticking up from your back pockets?
In a whirlwind of pollen, you-the-man
have seized you-the-woman to your breast
—his breast, her breast, tenderly, tenderly—
now you turn away and shyly grin.
Oh you possessors of youthful haircuts
& attractive activewear from L.L. Bean,
you whose buttocks are still small enough
to permit the rearview photograph:
don't you already have enough silver coinage
pouring from life's slot? But no, you also want
the river's silver surge where its bed drops off,
you want the namesake in all its glory—*Niagara:*
even the barge of animals teetering on its lip.
This ploy was wrought by some 19th-century huckster,
the honeymooners gathered on the shore's high bank
to watch the barge drop as creature-cries* rise up…
before all the couples re-bungalow themselves
to do what, then what, it's hard to imagine
after so much death. I always thought *Tigers*
until I read the barge was full of dogs and cats—
one baby camel, a demented old monkey,
la petite mort, that little French whimper
given up by the ordinary before it breaks into splinters.

The widow Taylor straps herself in a barrel
and rides it safely over the century's cusp,
& Maud Willard imbarrels herself with her dog
who'll leap from the busted staves alone.
Still, wouldn't the ride be worth that one live leap—
doesn't part of us *want* to be broken to bits?
After all, our bodies are what cage us,
what keep us, while, outside, the river
says more, wants more, is more: the *R*
(*grrrr, argh, graa…) in all its variegated coats.
A sound always coming, always smashing, always spoken
by the silver teeth and tongue that guard the river's open throat.

The Van with the Plane

At first I didn't get it: I thought it was just scrap metal roped on the roof
of this dented ancient Econoline van
with its parrot-yellow-colored burden.
Bright mishmash so precarious
my heart twitched whenever I had to tail it down the road
until one day I woke to it: you blockhead, that's a *plane*.

I don't know how I missed it—of course it was a plane,
disassembled, with one yellow wing pointing sideways from the roof.
Fuselage dinged by rocks from the road
and two little wheels sticking up from the van—
now when I tally all the pieces, it seems pretty obvious.
And I wonder if toting it around would be a burden

or more some kind of anti-burden.
Because if you drove around with a plane
you might feel less fettered than the rest of us:
say your life hung around your neck like a concrete Elizabethan ruff
you could always ditch that junker van
and take off rattling down the runway of the road.

But my friends said they'd seen that heap for so long on the road
it was like a knock-knock joke heard twice too often.
You'll be sorry they said when I went looking for the guy who drove the van,
whom I found in the library, beating the dead horse of his plane.
Once you got him started it was hard to shut him off:
how, if he had field to rise from, he'd fly to Sitka, or Corvallis—

but how does a guy living in a van get a field, you think the IRS
just goes around giving people fields for free? The road

of his thought was labyrinthine and sometimes ended in the rough
of Cambodia or Richard Nixon.
He said a plane in pieces still counts as a plane,
it was still a good plane, it was just a plane on a van.

And of course I liked him better as part and parcel of the van;
the actual guy could drive you nuts.
All his grace depended on his sitting underneath that plane
as it rattles up and down the road
like a train with a missile, a warhead of heavy hydrogen.
Because the van reverts to rubble once the plane takes off.

And if my own life is a plane, it's like the *Spirit of St. Louis* —
no windshield, just the vantage of a periscope.
Forward, onward, never look down — at the burden of these roofs and roads.

Snowstorm with Inmates and Dogs

The prison kennel's tin roof howls
while the dogs romp outside through the flakes.
The inmates trained a dog to lift my legs—
for months they rolled the concrete floor
in wheelchairs, simulating.

Through a window I watch them cartwheel now,
gray sweatpants rising against the whitened hill
traversed by wire asterisks and coils.
At first I feared they pitied me,
the way I flinched at the building's smell.

Now the tin roof howls, the lights go off
to the sound of locking doors. Go on, breathe—
no way the machinery of my lungs
is going to plow the county road.
Didn't I try to run over a guy,

spurned love being the kindling stick that rubbed
against his IOUs? Easy to land here,
anyone could—though I think laughter
would elude me, no matter what the weather.
Compared to calculating how far to the road.

Signs there say: CORRECTIONS CENTER DO NOT PICK UP HITCHHIKERS.
My instructions were: Accept no notes or photographs,
and restrict the conversation to such topics as
how to teach the dog to nudge
the light switch with his nose.

Now the women let their snowballs fly—as if
the past were a simple matter that could splat and melt.
Only my red dog turns his head
toward the pines beyond the final fence
before the generator chugs to life.

Early Cascade

I couldn't have waited. By the time you return
it would have rotted on the vine.
So I cut the first tomato into eighths,
salted the pieces in the dusk,
and found the flesh not mealy (like last year)
or bitter,
even when I swallowed the green crown of the stem
that made my throat feel dusty and warm.

Pah. I could have gagged on the sweetness.
The miser accused by her red sums.
Better had I eaten the dirt itself
on this the first night in my life
when I have not been too busy for my loneliness—
at last, it comes.

Twenty-five Thousand Volts per Inch

The weird summer of lightning (to be honest) was not a summer, but a week
when we sat every night in a far corner of the yard
to watch the silver twitch over our drinks.
It may help to know the sky hardly ever spasms here,
which is why we savored the postscript smell of nickel,
ions crisping in the deep fry.

The bolts made everything erogenous, the poppies and the pumpkin vine —
we could hardly bear to leave our watch post
but had tickets for the concert at the pier.
And we could not bear to miss the jam band from our youth,
which we feared discovering lacked talent and looked foolish
in their caveman belt buckles and leather hats.

Whew. That we found in them a soulfulness, an architecture
of tempo changes and chord progressions
left us relieved. Childishly
we hummed along as the sun got gulped down like a vitamin
and boats of cheapskates gathered on the bay.
When the lightning started, it was fearsome and silent

as usual. We were older, we knew this,
but the past proved not to be all suicide and motorcycle accidents.
Here was proof the music had shown some finesse —
even if it pillaged the discographies of black men from the Delta
it did so honorably, *erotically*, meaning
"that which gathers." So we held hands and drew near.

And the flashes lit us, when they lit us, in platinum flames:
then we saw, behold, below the bleachers,

a man whose rubber sneaker toe-tips
punctured the darkness as he spun.
He lurched and spun and lurched and fell,
a messenger from the ancient cults

until his stomach's contents were strobed ruthlessly
once they splattered on the tarmac. Sky says: *Rise,*
feet say: *Heavy.* Body would say: *Torn in two*
if it weren't already passed out
with all the good Samaritans busy remembering
the words to the tune about the rambling man. Oh

Bacchus, Dionysus, ye Southern rock stars
of antiquity: Thank you for shutting the black door
behind which he vanished, so we could resume
holding each other, like two swigs of mouthwash.
Then the brother who was not dead
played another of our childhood songs.

Tsunami Museum, Hilo

Because she comes here just a few hours a week, you are lucky
    to have found her—
Mrs. Ito, who is ninety-four: you have to bend way down
    and speak loudly in her ear.
To ask for the story she floats on these words: *wreckage* and *sky*,
    the wreckage and sky,
when she tells how her house lost its moorings at dawn
    to the shoulders of the surf.
How because she could not swim she clung to a door
    and rode it the night
of April Fool's Day, 1946:
    the whole seaward part of town destroyed.
So the museum sits now in the lee of the headland
    across from the bus station
where drunks sail to sleep on its wooden benches—
    the sun outside has fried them through.
Wreckage and sky, the turmoil and the clarity:
    timbers lobbed by the wave-crest
versus the constant stars. Or the wild hair of the drunks
    versus this morning's placid bay.
For sixty years she has sailed on the door
    of her story, and now she is sorry
she cannot tell it well enough—she left school to work
    in the hotdog plant
years before the wave. Yes,
    there were others who survived,
but they were children, so they were quick,
    outsprinting the surf—
they did not spend the night
    all stretched out on the sea.

Which was a deeper black than you could ever imagine,
    though what she says is:
All my friends are dead—
    not the wreckage, just the clarity
when you get to be so very old—*or in the hospital*
    with no brains left.
Only me, she says:
    she's the one who was saved.
And then she holds up her index finger, for you
    to throw your life ring on.

Driving Home from the Conference like a Pill with a Thousand People Inside

We turned off the highway at Chuckanut Drive
(everyone told us to turn off at Chuckanut Drive)
where, when we finally slid from the cedars,
the ocean smacked us in the face.
Jane squints down into her steering and talking
(her voice like the *hushing* of the wet road)
about how her mother fled from the house
(one of the many times he beat her).
How they wore their pajamas into the store
after crossing the parking-lot stripes in their slippers—
see how easy it is to start over
after the hangers screech.
In the motel, there'd always be a picture of the sea
(as if all you needed was the *idea* of its rocking)—
you feel your life starting over on Chuckanut Drive
(is what made Jane remember).
Our car crept like a grub on the country's edge,
there on a cliff above Samish Bay:
mountains to the north, mountains to the south,
(& a life equaled)
the huge unbroken water in between.

The Garbo Cloth

Her daughter wrote back to say my friend had died
    (my friend to whom I wrote a letter maybe twice a year).
From time to time I'd pictured her amid strange foliage
    (and in a Mongol yurt, for she was fond of travel).
Why not a flock of something darkening the sky, so we would know
    (*ah, so-and-so is gone!*)?
To a woman from the city, this might perhaps be pigeons
    (blacking out the sun).
Or else a human messenger, as once when she was fabric-shopping
    (bolt of green silk furled across her body)
Garbo passed, and nodded. At Macy's years ago
    (when I was not a creature in her world).
Of course she bought the cloth, but never sewed the dress
    ("a massive stroke, and I take comfort in the fact she felt no pain").
Logic says we should make omens of our Garbos and our birds
    (but which one bears the message? which one just the mess?).
From the kayak, I've seen pigeons nesting underneath the pier
    (a dim ammoniated stink)
where one flew into my face. I read this as a sign
    (that rancid smash of feathers)
but couldn't fathom what it meant, the bird trapped in the lag time
    (of an oracle's translation).
Foolish mind, wanting to obliterate the lag and why—
    (let memory wait to catch up to its sorrow).

In addition to the rattling of cellophane

What I remember about the famous writer is how
he took the English muffin sleeve from a high shelf,

how he mumbled his apologies
on finding only one stale white puck. How

he blew the cornmeal off
before he forked the halves apart, twisting to loosen them

the way my mother did.
How therefore came a little intermission of memory—

a patch of time he filled by pacing
in front of the toaster-oven window,

lacquered and leaded with grease
like the stained glass of a church.

How I was looking for wisdom, how he was no talker.
How he devoted himself instead to buttering,

palming the muffin-half close to his eye
while the golden glob vanished

into the craters.
How slowly he heaved it with his knife.

A Pedantry

Many of the great men—Buddha, Saint Augustine,
Jefferson, Einstein—had a woman and child
they needed to ditch. A little prologue
before the great accomplishments could happen.

From nothing came this bloody turnip
umbilicaled to the once-beloved,
only now she's transformed like a Hindu god
with an animal snout and too many limbs.

You'd rather board a steamer with chalk dust on your pants
or sit under a bo tree and be pelted by flaming rocks,
renounce the flesh
or ride off on a stallion—

there is no papoose designed for such purposes,
plus the baby would have to be sedated.
Sorry.
We don't want the future to fall into the hands of the wrong -ists!

That's how civilization came into being
for us who remained in the doorways of here,
our companions those kids who became chimney sweeps, car thieves,
and makers of lace.

By day we live in the shadows of theories; by night
the moon holds us in its regard
when it doesn't have more important business
on the back side of the clouds.

Four Red Zodiacs

Because I'd drunk a lot of coffee on top of some antibiotics
strange ideas were already swimming in my brain
like sharks patrolling their aquarium walls
when I saw those strange rafts circling in the harbor.

Gatling was the word that came to mind
for the machine guns mounted on their turrets,
but Jim said I was wrong. And also:
Great, so now the war comes to Palookaville

while I stood too stymied for a superior thought.
Eventually we turned back from the window
to our task to prove ourselves
not easily deterred:

loading the truck with bags of garbage
so we could take them to the dump.
Styrofoam boxes from the Vietnamese restaurants
by which we are sustained.

We came back dirty, so we washed,
then lay down predictably.
And it seemed oddly synchronous
that I'd just been reading Baudelaire,

who couldn't stand what sex did to the face. Meanwhile
a big ship slid into port
like a capsule sinking in the throat,
then some jeeps and earthmovers drove aboard.

And why not say *we fucked right through it!* —
an optimist might say that love prevailed.
But there is another way to look at it:
as greed, the body taking its cut first

(although I didn't look, I never can stand to look).

Later I thought I saw a frogman in the bay,
but it could have been a seal.
I mean a real seal,
which is to say an animal.

Then, Infamous Reader, comes your turn to say: *But we are all animals.*

Martha

Nearly all the remaining quarter million passenger
pigeons were killed in one day in 1896.

They named the last one Martha,
and she died September 1, 1914, in the Cincinnati Zoo,
she who was once one of so many billions
the sky went dark for days
when they flew past.
Makes me wonder what else could go,

some multitudinous widget like clouds or leaves
or the jellyfish ghosting the water in autumn
or the shore-shards of crushed clams?
Goodbye kisses:
once I had so many of you but now I note
your numbers growing slim —

yesterday a man stood me up in the sea
behind the big rock where the sand dollars live.
And when I said *Now we should kiss*
it seemed we'd grown too peculiar
and I thought: Oh-ho kisses, are you leaving too
like the man's hair? Or like

the taut bellies we once had
or the menstrual period that was mine alone —
time flew its coop
our days did skid
and now see my commas going too —
art mimicking life's mortal nature?

So I did no hem-haw with the man
I told him to grab hold of my ears
since daylight burned
the tide had begun to apply its suction then
the shotguns of our lips turned toward
what was perhaps the last of our wild flock.

Breaking News

for Hayden

They found the missing bride and she is living.
They found the boys floating on the ocean in their little yellow raft.
The ornithologists found the extinct woodpecker
when it flew over their canoe.
Not everyone is convinced, though.
One recording of its distinctive knock turned out to be a gunshot.

A century of Ozark fishermen
said they saw the bird when they were stranded
on their hummocks in the swamp.
Nobody believed them but the catfish in their pails.
Those boys thought their muscles strong enough to paddle against the squall.
And the bride only wanted a bus trip west
before the rest of her life downed her like an olive.

Sometimes survival strikes us dumb
with the improbable story of resurrection;
we see the blossoms smutted on the ground
turning back into a flowering tree. Next year
there'll be new nettle stalks
to sting your fingers, which you'll drag
through the scrrated leaves to prove
the world has not lost the consolation of its old pain.

For the First Crow with West Nile Virus to Arrive in Our State

For a long time you lay tipped on your side like a bicycle
but now your pedaling has stopped. Already
the mosquitoes have chugged their blisterful of blood
and flown on. Time moves forward,
no cause to weep, I keep reminding myself of this:
the body will accrue its symptoms. And the manuals of style
that warn us not to use the absolutes, are wrong:
the body will *always* accrue its symptoms.

But shouldn't there also be some hatchlings within view:
sufficient birth to countervail the death?
At least a zero on the bottom line:
I'm not asking for black integers,
just for nature not to drive our balance into the dirt.

What should we utter over the broken glass that marks your grave?
The bird books give us mating calls but not too many death songs.
And whereas the Jews have their Kaddish and the Tibetans
have their strident prayers, all I'm impelled to do is sweet-talk
the barricades of heaven. Where you my vector
soar already, a sore thumb among the clouds.

Still I can see in the denuded maple one of last year's nests
waiting to be filled again, a ragged mass of sticks.
Soon the splintered shells will fill it
as your new geeks claim the sky—any burgling
of bloodstreams starts when something yolky breaks.
And I write this as if language could give restitution for the breakage
or make you lift your head from its quilt of wayside trash.
Or retract the mosquito's proboscis, but that's language again,
whose five-dollar words not even can unmake you.

68

Not Winter

after reading Anne Carson's Sappho translation

How sad it must be in Greece when winter comes,
like Coney Island but with a less-brutal sea,
and what is sadder than a hot dog or souvlaki for that matter
when the last nub of meat slips through the bun
and the girls cover up their gowns so like translucent grocery sacks
caught spookily in trees and I think they're olive trees
only because I don't know much about Greece,
how do you expect me to know anything
when the papyri are in such tatters?
In all we have of Sappho's poems, the silences
come rolling forth like bowling balls:
blank after blank after blank after blank
[to remind us of what's missing].
Then comes a word like Gongyla or Gorgo,
which sounds like the name of a Japanese movie monster
instead of a girl too lovely
to be eating a hot dog made of useless lips.

But there is no food in Sappho's poems,
which makes me wonder about every other missing else,
who cooked the meat and carted off the chamber pots
so Sappho could stroll under the olive boughs so unencumbered
by her body, her reputedly squat wrestler's body,
thereby left free to strum her lyre? I am not saying
it is an easy thing to write a poem that will be remembered
for three thousand years, but it is a harder thing
to build a temple out of rocks. A temple
where the girls will party all-nite

until their gowns start flying off
and into that ferocious silence:
[   ].
Then comes two words intact—
I want

Love Swing

The new guy bought it as a present for his wife
(this a story Jim is telling)—
like a love swing like I think of as a love swing?
Jim uh-huhs: she'll ride it Christmas morn.
So let us stop to praise the new guy's paunch,
the dimpling in his wife's thighs,
though when I ask if *I* could ride a love swing
Jim says, "I'm afraid your love swing days are through."
In case of fire, strike chest with hammer
and wind up all the dogs in the neighborhood,
while I zen out trying to remember the name of… ah…
not Leland Stanford but *Stanford White*:
architect of Madison Square Garden,
where the famous velvet swing hung in his tower studio—
tapestries, sketches, photographs, a hive
of mammoth work and mammoth pleasure
all mashed together in one place.
But it was the swing
that drove jurors wild at the trial
where the killer named Thaw got off the hook
because his young bride Evelyn had ridden it,
laughing and kicking her dainty feet. And I think:
Maybe everybody in America has a love swing,
maybe it's as common as a jungle gym,
a secret no one has let me in on
until now, when it's too late. And my next thought
is that I have been all my life a tad repressed,
I mean I prided myself on having been around the block
but I never rode a love swing. Okay:
I've bought a costume or two at the department store

that also sells chopped meat and pineapples
where you hide the impractical straps and struts
between gardening gloves and a ream of typing paper
as they roll along the checkout's conveyor belt
where the bra gets dinged with grease.
But nothing requiring tools, nothing with such
ramifications: the kids pouncing on their bunk beds
while you're hammering away, I mean hanging it up
so you can kick a paper parasol like the one that Stanford White
hung from the ceiling: fiddle dee dee.
What about the giant hooks?
and Jim says you get two decoy ferns
in silk or plastic, so as not to get dirt on the carpet
and because you don't want to hang your love swing by the window
where a true living plant could grow.
The new guy bought it at the fantasy emporium
down by Pike Market, choosing the swing
over the hand-stitched ribbon underwear
sold in the boutique next door,
which cost a week's wages. Jim held out his arms
to indicate the way she'll hold the ropes—
a posture that made me think of Jesus,
forgive me for saying. But I'm so far gone
I can say anything: Hello Mister Death,
let's run this bar code through.
Ouch—
that love swing sets you back more than a hundred bucks,
but hey it's cheaper than the ribbons
and will give you years of sailing back and forth,
hanging from nothing but graveyard fog.
Mounting instructions are included
though they be written in Japanese,
and it even comes in a discreet black shopping bag
to match your—whatever you call it—
your robe your gown.

Altered Beast

You were a man and I used to be a woman
before we first put our quarters in

the game at the gas station, whose snack-chip display
wore a film of oil and soot

beside which you turned into a green gargoyle and then
a flying purple lynx—

whereas I could not get the hang of the joystick
and remained as I began

while you kicked my jaw and chopped my spine,
a beating I loved because it meant you were rising

fast through the levels—and the weak glom on
via defeat, which is better than nothing—

insert sound effects here: *blip blat ching ching*

…and when they stopped, your claws gripped the naked
-looking pink lizard that I was,

blood-striped and ragged, as if being a trophy
were the one reward the vanquished get—

which is why, walking home through the curbside sludge,
when you held my hand with your arm outstretched

as if you were holding a dripping scalp or head,
I hummed with joy to be your spoils.

Motorola

Silver moth whose wings flap before landing on the ear—
you stir the air with voices
and then a cloud swirls on the jet stream,
causing a typhoon a world away.
I am not happy about having to become a cell phone person,
even though I see the other cell phone people walking
with their necks bent so the sun can reach that lovely place below their ears.
I feel superior, listening to the juncos' aggravations
with you squirreled in a pocket on my breast
where you beep your ultimatums. That you have a molten look
makes me think that you could seep
into my body, so I'd contain multitudes
like Walt Whitman, all my friends alphabetized
along with the pain clinic, all ruled by that prim mistress
who asks for the codes and is so firm in her denials,
firm in her goodbye. I'd renounce her altogether
did my bones not have their exigencies—
when I fall, you give a little yawn as you unfold,
and then a fireman comes to lift me, muscles rumpling his rubber coat,
and I think that he will never age.
Why can't the mind simply roll around on its own wheels?
Why can't the body be rewired like a lamp?
The other cell phone people draw a thread through the world and stitch it close
whereas I go around huffing in a state of irritation
that I take to be the honest state of nature,
which is why I listen to the juncos, though it's difficult to decode their words.
And though I hold you, Moth, in my contempt, I've spoken through you
for enough minutes from what the corporation calls *my plan*
that your numbers have become infused with my mouth's smell.
It is not the junco's bird-smell of vinegar and berries

but that person-smell of roasted meat and sweat,
and I could spray you with disinfectant but that would fry your circuitry—
to wipe away the human would make you go kaput.

On the Chehalis River

All day long the sun is busy, going up and going down,
and the moon is busy, swinging the lasso of its gravity.
And the clouds are busy, metamorphing as they skid—
the vultures are busy, circling in their kettle.

And the river is busy filling up my britches
as I sit meditating in the shallows until my legs go numb.
Upstream I saw salmon arching half into the air:
glossy slabs of muscle I first thought were seals.

They roiled in a deeper pocket of the river,
snagged in a drift net on Indian land.
Trying to leap free before relenting to the net
with a whack of final protest from the battered tail.

They'll be clubbed, I know, when the net's hauled up
but if there were no net they'd die anyway when they breed.
You wonder how it *feels* to them: their ardent drive upstream.
What message is delivered when the eggs release.

A heron sums a theory with one crude croak; the swallows
write page after page of cursive in the air. My own offering
is woozy because when their bodies breached the surface
the sun lit them with a flash that left me blind.

Number One

for Ben

Animal attack is Number One in the list called
"Ways in Which I Do Not Want to Die" —
wait, Ben says knock it off with the death-talk;
you've already talked death to death.

But the Number Ones don't need our speech
to claim their cool dark storage place: my sister said
hers was falling down the stairs, after her husband left
and every riser turned into El Capitan.

Sleeping on the sofa did nothing about the steps
connecting the world to her front porch. Three is more
than enough, given a new moon and tallow on the instep
and the right force-vectors applied to the neck.

I said *Relax, you should join a health club*
so my sister rowed until she withered to a twig,
and when the office microfiche clerk *did* fall down the stairs
all that hemoglobin on the cellar floor

sent my sister's paw back to her popcorn bowl
as she asked the darkness from a fetal pose
about the safety of a pup tent
set up in a housing tract.

Thus do our Number Ones sit on our chests
like sumo wrestlers in lifeboats — rowing rowing.
And some nights in my phantasmagloriland
I am supped by shark or dingo dog or a cannibal king.

Then I am a movie star (if not your classic movie star),
just one of the shriekers who is always beautiful
when her head spins suddenly
and her hair fans.

And what could Numbers Seven or Twelve offer by compare:
those falling-elevator dreams
the fire dreams
the riptide dreams

the dreams of death as a mere phenomenon of weather?
I know my celebrity is fleeting as I thrash and holler and yet
see the moviegoers prick up in their seats:
see the good it does,

how it is not so grim or tragic
when the boy-hand spiders across girl-shouldermeat
and she curls against him
like a pink prawn thawing from the freezer.

Then his hand goes tumbling to her breast—
you see what magic I am giving them
astir in frumpy velvet seats arrayed in front of my disquiet
at this brink this moment when she lets it stay.

Bert Wilson Plays Jim Pepper's "Witchi-Tai-To" at the Midnight Sun

Don't look up, because the ceiling is suffering
some serious violations of the electrical code,
the whole chaotic kelplike mess
about to shower us with flames.
I think I can render this clearly enough —

Bert's saxophone hanging between his knees,
propped against the wheelchair's seat
where his body keeps shape-shifting —
he's Buddha then shop-vac then Buddha again,
formlessness floating on top of form.

The problem is backstory, how to get it all in,
not just Bert's beanie and tie-dye T-shirt,
but polio too, and the tune itself, concentric ripples
widening. So now I send dead Jim Pepper
rippling out, as well as his grandfather,

fancy-dancing and chanting. How to tender
the lead-in, would phonemes do any good
(the signature *DAHH*, the *doon doons* down-marching) —
or just call it a prayer to simplify things
as Bert sends the melody way out

beyond the tidiness of circles?
Then he puts the mouthpiece aside
to bring up the words from the floor of his soul
or say from the pads of his spud-shaped feet
spraddling the footplate, if *soul* is too hokey

for all the misty goo inside us.
First comes the Creek part of the song
and then comes the English, when Bert throws back his chin:
his underbeard raised in a coyote salute
to the water infusing the warehouse roof.

Here, take a seat on these rickety risers
inside my head, though your life isn't mine,
still, I have hope for your hearing
the gist of this refrain
about how glad he is that he's not dead.

Accidental Dismemberment

From Hartford, from Allentown, they used to send their letters —
the corporate stationery featured the word *LIFE*.
Somewhere radio towers twinked
and garters held up the socks of men
whose fine print said that if I ever lost my arm in a buzz-saw accident —
boy, that would be the day my ship came in.

So I pictured myself shopping for produce with my feet,
a melon riding on my tarsal bones and money
smoking in my pocket. But this dream-trafficking gave way
to wondering what it took to land in jail —
for steady meals and solitude
and a tin cup to play the bars like a marimba!

You might need enough time to write a book as long as Proust's,
yet not so much to fire up the chair they call *Ol' Sparky:*
so we're talking a fine calibration here. To elsewhere
my love and I will be speeding in the car
when he'll clap his ears: *Stop I can't stand any more this Looosha talk!*
leaving the steering wheel dangerously unattended

though I tell him many writers think about the hoosegow
as a meditative place. Especially now
when the junk mail comes in photon blips,
say from Mrs. Mobutu Sese Seko needing a little cash to tide her over
and spokespersons for the penis you have to wind on a wheel
like a garden hose. What insurance executive

walks to work anymore while dreaming
up fine print for my lost feet?

There is much to envy in that woman
who flaunts her perfect body on the Key West shore—
yet five thousand dollars still seems like a lot of money,
especially for one of these fingers I don't use much.

Inseminating the Elephant

The zoologists who came from Germany
wore bicycle helmets and protective rubber suits.
So as not to be soiled by substances
that alchemize to produce laughter in the human species;
how does that work biochemically is a question
whose answer I have not found yet. But these are men
whose language requires difficult conjugations under any circumstance:
first, there's the matter of the enema, which ought to come
as no surprise. Because what the news brings us
is often wheelbarrows of dung—suffering,
with photographs. And so long as there is suffering,
there should be also baby elephants—especially this messy,
headlamp-lit calling-forth. The problem lies
in deciding which side to side with: it is natural
to choose the giant rectal thermometer
over the twisted human form,
but is there something cowardly in that comic swerve?
Hurry an elephant
to carry the bundle of my pains,
another with shiny clamps and calipers
and the anodyne of laughter. So there, now I've alluded
to my body that grows ever more inert—better not overdo
lest you get scared; the sorrowing world
is way too big. How the zoologists start
is by facing the mirror of her flanks,
that foreboding luscious place where the gray hide
gives way to a zeroing-in of skin as vulnerable as an orchid.
Which is the place to enter, provided you are brave,
brave enough to insert your laser-guided camera
to avoid the two false openings of her "vestibule,"

much like the way of entering death, of giving birth to death,
calling it forth as described in the Tibetan Book.
And are you brave enough to side with laughter
if I face my purplish, raw reflection
and attempt the difficult entry of that chamber where
the seed-pearl of my farce and equally opalescent sorrow
lie waiting?

For the Mad Cow in Tenino

I don't know where you rank in my list of killers:
my viral load, my sociopaths, my inattention
on the interstate, where I crane my head after the hawk
and the windshield splatters
into diamonds. Not just thinking about the hawk,
or even merely watching it, I always have to *be* it for a minute,
just as my mind enters the murderers
for one long flash before it stumbles out.

From your postmortem, you held us fast
while a man said *It's enough* as his lungs filled
after being stabbed here near the playground,
before they milled his limbs with power tools
and scattered him beyond retrieval. Too late
to recall your brain, and the fatty white part of your spine,
already delivered to the rendering plant
and melted down into the slurry.

That night is gone and cannot be reassembled
despite my re-imagining the car
with a man dying in its trunk, a car otherwise like any other,
as we could not verify your affliction
for days after you fell. Which left the land in chaos
except for Scatter Creek's flowing past,
wending without hurry though the coastal range
before it empties rain and blood into Willapa Bay.

Garfield's Dream

Should we not know that James Garfield suffered from crippling writer's block and simply could not finish his speech until 2:30 on the morning of the inaugural? As the day approached, he had an anxiety dream in which he fell off a canal boat and was suddenly standing naked in the wilderness during a wild storm. After finding a few pieces of cloth to cover himself and embarking on "a long and tangled journey," he found his way to a house where "an old negro woman took me into her arms and nursed me as though I were a sick child." Comforted, he awoke to face his presidency.

TED WIDMER, *The American Scholar*, WINTER 2005

Start with one cell, call it a zygote,
call it a diploid that turns into me—fool, petunia, witch.
Samaritan and crow. Endless nouns
I could plug in. And yet my eye
can be told from the world's other billions of eyeballs
by machines that map the galaxy
of specks and glints that make up its blue ring.

Then how to account for Garfield's dream
being the same one I've dreamed,
except the old woman had a child and the child held a doll
who was a replica of the child?
I think there's a me in a black veil
who has dreamed it, too
(because the crow is a fool because the witch will presume),
as well as a me who'll strap explosives to his chest
tomorrow, when he'll blow himself back
into the disarray of cells.
Dear Assassin:
stay here with me in the dream—
we have only a few more hours of night
to be held together by neither our wife's nor our mother's arms.

Sylvia Plath's Hair

for Marianne Boruch

In Bloomington, Indiana, the librarian lugged it from the archive
    in a cardboard box, the kind that long-stemmed roses come in—
there was even tissue paper she unfolded
    like someone parting a lover's blouse
or like the skin of a corpse being peeled by a pathologist,
    this librarian who wore white gloves
when she poked her eraser at the braid as if it might explode.

And I made a mental note to write but could not decide if I should start
    with the waxy clots of follicle, or the bristle of split ends—
what word to describe the loose strands' electrostatic web?
    I start to write and wander into the tangle of my wondering
whatever happened to that yellow paper-mâché horse
    displayed in our dining room where I grew from my pogo stick
into my humid secondary sexual characteristics?

Now it must fertilize a flower bed in some suburban subdivision
    erected over the detoxified county dump.
Where rot the archives of the childhoods that we see
    our therapists either to remember or to forget.
Because who has as much faith in the past as Sylvia Plath's mother—
    not to mention the muscle mass to lift the boxes?
And how many women leave Bloomington

with plans to write about the hair, which had a hint of purple
    like the fuzz extruding from a thistle
when the flower after-blossoms on the green pineapplish nub?
    Across America, women wad their paper asteroids

while dusty stallions are being pitched into the trash.
    Pitched by widows moving into condominiums
because their daughters have skipped town. And we wonder

if they were just faking their pride in our poor creations,
    with legs like bratwursts because I grew too excited
applying the paper strips like a trauma nurse.
    Oh we are daughters without daddies
or sufficient antihistamines, drifting off to Bloomington
    like spent weeds combing through the air.
Which reminds me — as per the static — how could I have lost it,

that word *flyaway*.

Trade Surplus

The whole waiting room
(Neurology Unit, seventh floor)
watches the balloon climb through the city, then turn
down a corridor leading to the sea.

Everyone looks.
And is joined in consensus
about the Happy Objects, overruling all elections.
Even the bad news does not come, not yet.

Later, the freeway:
when the dildo-franchise delivery truck speeds up
with two people painted on its side, sitting in bed
under the halos of their blissed-out brains —

I hoist my thumb like a good citizen.
But the driver has been trained by the corporation
(with a trendy slice of mirror on his eyes)
to sourpuss the glee through which he trolls his simulated genitalia.

Today the inanimate world rises up against him
as it hums without its batteries,
humming louder than the lightboard
where my cerebellum revealed its zones of mist

and its granules of (*very bad*) dark matter
over which Dr. Kita ran her lovely fingers.

Sixty miles, seven hawks,
after curling down the off-ramp

when the blue T. rex out front of Done-Rite Automotive
suddenly drops its head—

only then am I jabbed by one sharp astral needle.
Until the beast deflates
enough to reveal two men in the process of unpinioning
that vinyl dino with their greasy fingers.

Another day shot, death one spin closer
like the slice of pie that any luck might slide their way—
T. rex exhales one last blue breath,
and when the black palms wave, I wave.

About the Author

Lucia Perillo grew up in the suburbs of New York City in the 1960s. She graduated from McGill University in Montreal in 1979 with a major in wildlife management and subsequently worked for the U.S. Fish and Wildlife Service. She then completed her M.A. in English at Syracuse University while working seasonally at Mount Rainier National Park.

In 1987 she moved to Olympia, Washington, where she taught at Saint Martin's College. For most of the 1990s Perillo taught in the creative writing program at Southern Illinois University. She now lives back in Olympia with her husband and dog.

Lannan Literary Selections

For two decades Lannan Foundation has supported the publication and distribution of exceptional literary works. Copper Canyon Press gratefully acknowledges their support.

LANNAN LITERARY SELECTIONS 2009

Michael Dickman, *The End of the West*

James Galvin, *As Is*

Heather McHugh, *Upgraded to Serious*

Lucia Perillo, *Inseminating the Elephant*

Connie Wanek, *On Speaking Terms*

RECENT LANNAN LITERARY SELECTIONS
FROM COPPER CANYON PRESS

Lars Gustafsson, *A Time in Xanadu,* translated by John Irons

David Huerta, *Before Saying Any of the Great Words: Selected Poems,*
translated by Mark Schafer

June Jordan, *Directed by Desire: The Collected Poems*

Sarah Lindsay, *Twigs and Knucklebones*

W.S. Merwin, *Migration: New & Selected Poems*

Valzhyna Mort, *Factory of Tears,* translated by Franz Wright
and Elizabeth Oehlkers Wright

Taha Muhammad Ali, *So What: New & Selected Poems, 1971–2005,*
translated by Peter Cole, Yahya Hijazi, and Gabriel Levin

Dennis O'Driscoll, *Reality Check*

Kenneth Rexroth, *The Complete Poems of Kenneth Rexroth*

Ruth Stone, *In the Next Galaxy*

C.D. Wright, *One Big Self: An Investigation*

Matthew Zapruder, *The Pajamaist*

For a complete list of Lannan Literary Selections from Copper Canyon Press, please visit Partners on our Web site:

www.coppercanyonpress.org

The Chinese character for poetry is made up of two parts: "word" and "temple." It also serves as pressmark for Copper Canyon Press.

Since 1972, Copper Canyon Press has fostered the work of emerging, established, and world-renowned poets for an expanding audience. The Press thrives with the generous patronage of readers, writers, booksellers, librarians, teachers, students, and funders—everyone who shares the belief that poetry is vital to language and living.

Major funding has been provided by:

Anonymous

Beroz Ferrell & The Point, LLC

Cynthia Hartwig and Tom Booster

Lannan Foundation

National Endowment for the Arts

Cynthia Lovelace Sears and Frank Buxton

Washington State Arts Commission

For information and catalogs:

COPPER CANYON PRESS
Post Office Box 271
Port Townsend, Washington 98368
360-385-4925
www.coppercanyonpress.org

This book is set in Electra, created by American typographer and book designer
W.A. Dwiggins in 1935. Book design by Valerie Brewster, Scribe Typography.
Printed on archival-quality paper at McNaughton & Gunn, Inc.